# The Darkness is Vanishing

# The Darkness is Vanishing

**Ramesh Pokhriyal 'Nishank'**

Translated by
**Dr. Chetana Pokhriyal**

**PRABHAT PRAKASHAN**
ISO 9001: 2015 Publishers

*Published by*
**PRABHAT PRAKASHAN**
4/19 Asaf Ali Road,
New Delhi-110 002 (INDIA)
Tele : +91-11-23289777
e-mail: prabhatbooks@gmail.com

ISBN 978-93-5322-768-5
**THE DARKNESS IS VANISHING**
Poems *by* Ramesh Pokhriyal 'Nishank'

*Edition*
First, 2020

*Price*
₹ 300.00 (Rupees Three Hundred only)



*Printed at*
R-Tech Offset Printers, Delhi

# Preface

'What is it all about' is all that I wondered when I naturally picked up a collection of small poems *Andhera Ja Raha Hai* by Shri Ramesh Pokhriyal Nishank for translation into English. While translating his work, I came across an ardent literature with well-depicted literary aesthetics within a politician known for his astute decisions in public arena. While translating 138 poems from this collection, his religious faith, sensitivity, wisdom, spirituality and philosophy of life, which resonated as a balm to the restless spirit and devotedness in his poems has not been a relaxed mission but an ardent endeavour. What captured my attention and the will to translate were the innate passionate ramifications and poetical mystification to the readers, which might include hymns singing and religious instructions, but what cannot be missed is the sentimental piety of the poems that he offers in this collection. As a poet, Nishank surveys the possibilities, compares them to the actualities, facts, theories, the alternatives and the ideal, and weighs them together. Hence, they are both insightful and foresighted to make a sense of worth of life. Amazing is the fact, that these poems are not complex but simple and pliable and the doctrines and practices endorsed in them are not something new and recent but in tandem with the established norms. Nishank is a highlander from the state of Uttarakhand and hence, most of his poems gain repertory or the popular consciousness of the native state, the voices and the romantic aura that he raises now in favour of the humanist attains general currency as a new concept of experience portraying an intellectually driven genius. The lyric quality of Nishank's poems displays the compressed and non-narrative structure as well as their melodramatic prominence. This compression and the quality shared by the lyric poem, heightens the direct intense projections of emotions, which is so characteristic of his poems.

Nishank conceives a probability in the law of nature supplementing it with the limitations inherent in the experiences. However, they emerge as something intrinsic, indigenous and something, which is intertwined together with the sentences, the structure, and texture and tone-so that anybody who reads it realises.

The collection of poems in *The Darkness is Vanishing* stirs the spirit or make our hearts dance and come over us like a mystical suppleness in a mood that is enchanting enough to pacify the distressed feelings refreshingly and absorbs within a sense of truth, clarity and refinement. While his poem

‘Relations’ reflects on the basic human emotions of honesty and faith intrinsic for any relations, he moors over the basic fundaments of true friendship in his four-liner poem ‘Friendship’. They are meditative and not obsessively zealous and packed with an acumen of a visionary and tenderness. The poet rather than projecting the flights of imagination and fantasy refrains from the overwhelming surges of emotional outburst and prefers to mould them into grace. The themes of most of his poems revolve around human life and emotions, which is not only the subject of all his poems but the great centre and sources of all interest in all periphery of all work where human being exists. At other places, Nishank croons his resilience to fight life rather than accept defeat in ‘Will Not Accept Defeat’. His poems are successful in riveting our attention and rousing our emotions. Nishank conjures the image of common place, every day and affable life of socially intellectual and passionate men who dance, croon, and fall but rise, shortly devastated but soon resilient. However, they do not contain any stories and no human characters. His poems are popularly and peculiarly contemplative. The poet conjures up the metaphoric story of Lord Krishna and Sudama in ‘Love is Strong’ while in the other ‘Need Paarth’ the intrinsic relation that existed between Lord Krishna and the legendary archer Arjuna to weave a sacred bond of love and friendship. For example, in ‘Need Paarth’, Nishank adheres to the belief in the path of enlightenment, a course of action recommended by Lord Krishna to Arjuna. The Poet reflects on the intrinsic role played by Arjuna in a cosmic mission to establish the structures of faith, hope, action, renunciation from sins, adherence to truth and honesty in a society. Hence, the poet invokes the spirit of Arjuna, who symbolises true devotion to accept the teachings of Lord Krishna willingly with faith.

In short, even in the profoundest poems, Nishank has a mastery to control the tone of the poems, which is the tone of true perception and worldly wisdom, true virtue and the poems are the expression of the longer experience, and more extended views. However, his verses are the greater favourites with both the old and the new alike. The literary charisma of his efforts is similar to its ethical charm and the panache of the diction is as indulgent, elegant, graceful and artless in tandem with the sentiments, which is plentiful and genuine. Poets and philosophers have used darkness across the globe as a metaphor to invoke the feelings of despair and gloom. Nishank dispels the feeling of helplessness by invoking the spirit of light, a binary opposite of darkness and can only be propelled through the teachings of *The Bhagavad Gita so that* 'the showers of happiness will descend that world' in his poem 'Remove Darkness, Erase Sorrows'. *The Bhagavad Gita* is the quintessential Hindu classical text with a very well laid out charter for human actions whether political or social and is frequently referred to not only by the Hindus but scholars globally. The poet invokes the spirit of *Dharma* inherent within the collective Indian consciousness and can be roughly translated as religion, duty, morality, justice, law and order within the cultural structures of establishing human society on solid moral foundation. Nishank successfully aspires to build the structures of faith and hope with the deep-rooted spiritual traditions for the development of the higher truth through this collection.

Everywhere in the educational, literary and political world, Nishank talks of missions, a direction with a sharp sense of purpose without ever losing sight of embarking on the values of humanity *per se*. The book is an offering to the readers with emphasis on the thoroughgoing changes in the universe and within him simultaneously. Lying within the sphere of sense, feeling and thought is the dogmatic belief that is hemmed in the human instincts for the preservation and expression of the human self. However, the dogmas are not closed or antagonistic to the practical approach to the universal creeds. The romantic analogy in *The Darkness is Vanishing* identifies everything that is Good with the universal principles of Truth and Beauty. Nishank, in his poetic endeavour to embark upon the fundamental problems of life to gather the ideas, correlate them, and patch up a system of realistic idealism with frequent touches of mysticism and the human nature struggles with life with trust in God. The presence of the immanent divinity within is the true purpose of human existence and the representation of God.

**—Chetana Pokhriyal**
Associate Professor & Head
Department of English
MKP PG College
Dehradun

# Contents

# My Words

I have a belief —
My emotions in my words
In the latent lifelessness
Will kindle the love for life
In a sleeping asleep lost mind
Will kindle the passion of something to do.

□

## Relations

To redeem the relations
Where one has to take the oath
Where one has to take the pledge
Is taxing.
Relations only needs
Honesty, faith and
Moreover, rationality.

□

## Friendship

It is not the friendship, which is sacred
The performer is,
In a friendship, a non- performer
Remains alone at the crossing.

□

## Keep Protected

Have not forgotten
Nor can forget
Their memories
Warily keep protected,
However
Many moments of life there are
Where they barge like a storm,
Raising the wall of trouble
In the mind
Rise up the storm.

□

## Dreamer of Songs

Immortal dream songs
I will not let miss
Lit the fire in every haunt
Let not the malice to sow.

□

# Will Not Accept Defeat

Know that it is decided
I will bring spring
Will dedicate everything
However will not accept defeat.

## The Spring

If you exist in me
I will have artless living
That which is created every moment
That spring will be self-created.

□

## For Your Sake

The tyranny of time and tide
Was no less to knock me down.
Nevertheless, I still
Lived remembering you.
The world has venom mixed
By all and sundry on my track.
Nevertheless, I remained tight-lipped
Downing the poison.

□

## The Reason

By becoming the minarets of memories
In perishing and splitting
Lose not the relations.
That becomes
The reason to survive
Thus are some specific relations.

□

## Memories

Not elapsed even once
Even for a moment
The promises that I have made to you
Where all
And in what way
I have veiled
Your memories within.

□

## To Smile

To smile in life
A motive is desired
Customary is smiling in crowd
But reason for happiness in heart
Is desired.
Looking happy in the frame
Is easy, but
In reality in life
Something should mesmerise.
The frolicking and chuckling life
Is only other way to live
The cynical storm out in lamentation
Is the outcome of their life.

□

## Mystery

The flow of tears
Has its own knack
When in happiness
And, when in grief
Is a deep mystery in itself.

□

## Whose Meeting

Whose meeting
Brings happiness to life
Even if we sought them after.
Is very difficult to get
Whose toil
Make even withered buds blossom
Even in sadness and pain
Only their faces bloom.

□

## The Placid

The depth of the placid
To the unbeknown queries
Replies mutely
Enduring peace, without saying anything
Every sadness and pain
Conceals in the heart

□

## Made for Others

Those created
To give happiness to others
Indeciduous are they.
Nor do they assent to
The loss of any life
Nor their own.

□

## Your Deals

Even your deals
Are somewhat strange
Which is
A destiny only to some.
With a shower of
Your slightest smile
You win over us
For life.

□

## Let There Be a Rain of Happiness

Be always happy
Let there be a breeze of success
You just sail in that.
To even the farthest
Let there be no gloom of pain.
Where there is
Rain of happiness
That
Beautiful fascinating
Pleasant be your town.

□

## Breeze

May this bouquet
Fill fragrance in your life,
Every feather like sweet fragrant breeze
Veil over water, earth and sky.

□

## Creativity

Come walk with me
So that even I
Aspire to grasp the summit
For a new world
A new destination
For new age will be created.

□

# A Beautiful Idea

Life is beautiful
Love it aplenty
Live on this
Perish for others.
This life
A renewed feeling
Provides you with
Just close your eyes
A deep breath
Take
To live a life
Commit to a beautiful idea.

□

# A Pledge

Life has now
Evoked
Happiness,
So that the complete
World be grasped within the arms
Is my whole dream.
To perfume
The flowers
Is the pledge I have taken
Now even
The bristles
Are holding on to my lappet.

□

## The Juice of Nectar

To support the tree
Minute roots
Are responsible.
Even the minutest roots
Have a role to play
In the care of this tree.
In this immortal consciousness
Life's new-fangled sapling sprouts
With the strength of the roots
It is not uprooted even in the storm.

□

## Not Even by Mistake

To save our tears from infamy
Gently
Conceal, them in your lappet
If at all by mistake
You somehow muse
Just crave to meet.

□

## Few Memories

Few memories
With smile
Also tears
Evoke.
Few memories
From past to the present reality
Conjure.

□

## Love is Strong

Love is very strong
If you can understand
Its immense power
Feel it to the core.
Only love is strong
To bend the world
If not then why
Lord Krishna
Rinsed Sudama's feet
With his tears.

□

## Need Paarth

In a journey of life
A togetherness of all we need
In staggering pathways
A helping hand of one another is needed.
Life though may get over
Wandering through the woodland in solitude
For walking on the right path
Each their own chaperon longs for.

□

## More Closely

We solely kept
Looking at each other
Together we flowed through
Feelings of the other;
A new dawn will arrive
Breaking through our darkness
To cause genuine smiles.

Our sorrows and
Happiness then will unite
Their soft realisation
Will then bring us more close.

□

# One Day Then

In the midst of any sorrow
Keep smiling
Whatever anguishes in the world be
Smile to endure,
The darkness will cease
Smile
Emerge will the new dawn.

□

# Be the Cloud

Again, emerge like a spring tide
Becoming light in my life
Anonymously into the mist of darkness
Disappear not
Instead of greenery
Autumn fetch not
The earth is yearning
Instead be the clouds
To quench its heat.

□

## The Gift

Simple it is to ally
But to remain lifelong aligned is a challenge
To be together and with its belief
Ceaselessly moving ahead.
This is life
Philosophy of minutest things,
A life full of happiness
The gift of this togetherness.

□

# I am Coming

As a vessel
I am reaching you
For you
I am bringing
A ray of hope.
To prevent you from drowning,
By giving my life
This assurance from god
Will for sure yield.

□

## In Your Arms

Welcome your God with eyes closed
Make a solicitous plea with a purposive mind.
Embracing his celestial image within
Love him from the depth of the soul.
Realise you will then
The sail through the beauty of the track
Open your eyes to realise
The bright world in your arms.

□

## Peak Goals

With him
The memories of perpetual relations
Generates
Integrality and intimacy
And
Intimacy!
In that infinite
Packs love.
The love
That is
The peak goal of life.

□

## Hard Work

The dynamos of hard work
No obstacles can stop,
Where goes the caravan of labour
Success follows with speed.

□

## Remove Darkness, Erase Sorrows

Its sorrows I care not
Even if darkness is all spread out
Singe the self
Fetch the bright light
Erase the blackness from the orb,
I will go to the skyline
Reach every particle for the benefice of the masses
Sing chants from the Gita,
Where there are the showers of happiness
Will descend that world.

□

## Belief

All those who believe in themselves
Only their destiny rises
Incessant practice and vigorous efforts solely
Can change providence.

□

# Efforts

True that success
Awaits efforts,
Sweet are the fruits of those efforts
Reside that in persistent desires.

□

## The Mystery

Only self-toil can for human
Raise the latent destiny
Only self-thinking, explores the secrecy
Of evolution.

□

## I am a Burning Lamp

I am a burning lamp, I burn
To erase all gloom,
Behold! the tyranny of the air
Impending with intent to blow me out.

□

## A Thought

The thinking of man
Differentiates him
From the crowd of the world,
Good thinking
Always remains alive
For which the world dies.

□

# Identity

Oh! Yes!
Every human voice
Is his identity
And
Utterances and upright in a voice
Are its garb.
Whosoever hears
Can make a conjecture.
Human!
With his voice and humility
Not only in the world,
Extend can
Even beyond the horizon.

□

## Let Speak

Hidden behind his voice
Is every man,
Let the doors of the heart open
If you want to understand
His character
Let them speak something.

□

## Snake Charmer

Snake charmer is sad
Raising snakes
Started to escape,
Now instead of snakes
Its now the man
Who stings.

□

## Vulture

Stunned by its destiny
The man appears to be
Seeing this all the vulture also
Has started crying.
Ponders
Why am I on the ground
When human
Razes the human.

□

## Made of Stone

Heard that this
Body is made of clay
One day
To be blended in the soil,
Came empty handed
Will go empty-handed.
In this journey called life
Such coincidences met,
Not so much of soil though
Met people turning into stones.

□

## Relationship of Money

Proud he was
When money he had
From the hurricane of time
All relationships are lost,
When in pocket an eyelet surfaced
All with money
Relationships too slide.

□

## Silences

Concealed your deeds
Staying in silence
Cloaked your sorrows
Confiding in your heart.

□

## Taught Many Lessons

What books could not teach me
All my life,
I looked at every face
Found not only books
But epics.
Those faces to me
Have revealed the reality of the world,
Those same faces
Have shown a lot in life
These faces in life
Have taught many lessons.

□

## Courage

Always staying with you
This encouragement enhances you
Whatever is in mind
Anyways make it happen.

□

## Passion

Your passion
Makes every work
Only passion teaches to run
Passion only fills
Causes to glide.
There is a unique relationship
Between mind, desire and passion
What you cannot do
That passion
Makes you do.

□

## Identification of That Person

Nor caste nor creed
Nor race nor distinction
No class, no colour is there
Ideal are devoid of rituals
Sweet love is the ritual
The gift of life by god
All are here bound by love
Unity in diversity
Where love is
Those who die for humanity
Great is that man.

□

## Difference

If any of you
See someone small
So in your eyes
There is some difference
Every person is self-specific
What is the matter with you?
Stout length like a date
What life is to live,
The robes on the body
Not crow bar but sown only by the needle.

□

# First

Keep high aim
Have patience
Every moment is precious
Understand the significance of these moments
Before doing anything
Do self-thinking
And then -
To execute your thinking
Take flight of confidence.

□

## Our Own Path

One who try teaching others
They hang in balance,
Finding faults in others for a while
Wander from their own path.

□

## Dust the Mistakes

Putting dust on the mistakes
Is bad,
They one after the other
Sows all the problems.
Man in this dust
Loses its power,
If there is dust on the face
Then there is no
Fault with the glass.

□

## Desperate

Even competent snake charmer
Cannot remove
Hidden snakes
In the sleeves,
For being unable to remove, poison from
Human fangs
Appears desperate.

□

## Had We Been Strong

Those who are strong
Toiling, move ahead
On their path,
Not too afraid of the terrible winds.
Whose roots
Are deep and deep
They do not shake even in big storms.

□

# Cannot Happen

Keeping oneself alive
In the crowd of the world
Cannot be lost,
They
Will not reach their destination
It cannot happen.

□

## They Never Extinguish

To erase the darkness
Who themselves
Burn like torches
Even in the adverse torrents
They never douse.

□

# Truth

Hiding truth
Is not difficult
Is impossible,
Even though
You dishonor someone
Or apply false accusations.
But one day
Truth will be out
The conspirator
Because of his own misdeeds
Will suffer defeat.

□

# Thought

Frivolous thinking
Makes man small
At every level
Fills man with narrow-mindedness
Raises doubts of
All types.
However, when thinking is big
Then it is a solution
Of every problem.

□

## Body and Mind

To have only fair skin is not enough
It is necessary
The mind of man
Is also fair
Let there be no
Soot of notoriety
Every page of my heart
Should be blank.

□

# Arrogance

'I am the best'
It can be
Self-confidence.
However, 'only I am the best'
One who says this
Can never grow bigger
Due to this ego
Only and only
Laments for the self,
At every intersection
He remains just lonely.

□

## Will Open the Secret

Not used to
To strike behind the back
Not used to
To fight against anyone unnecessarily.
We
Whatever will speak, speak in front
For the benefit of others
Will not open the hidden secrets.

□

## True Happiness

Truth has its own pleasure
There is rapture in it to live life
It is a little hard way, but
These are the colours of excitement, and fidelity,
From here the purity
Of the soul begins
Which cleanses all the meanness.

□

## The Passion of Success

The passion for success
Is mandatory
The difficulties
Will duck down in some corner,
With difficulties
If you are unnerved in life
Spent it in lamentation.

□

## The Errands of Life

In running errands for life
Where are we bound to
Nobody could know,
Ephemeral respite is momentary
Nobody believed.

□

## In Me

I have a mind in me
Corporal in me,
It is also excitement
Sorrows in me too.
The path in me
The journey within,
The world in me
The destination inside,
Why worried?
When everything is in me

□

## Also of Others

Like the rising sun
The sharpness is to be increased
To increase it
Will have to inure the self.
In the sharpness of the sun
You can only see yourself,
From the light inside
You can remove
The darkness of others.

□

## Money or Knowledge

Earning money only
And with the aim to protect it
To absorb life
Is to turn away from life.
Be worthy
In every moment of your life
Need to add new achievements.
No need to earn knowledge
And protect it
Knowledge will protect you
Whether you stay here or somewhere.

□

# A Lesson

If you learn lessons
From mistakes,
You will come back
Refreshed,
And if lessons
Not learnt
You will make
Mistakes again and again
And suffer
Worst damages in each stride.

□

## The Prick

Feel the prick
It will
Make you vigilant,
Making you capable
Will create surrender in you.
This prick will
Make you strong
In vexing circumstances
Will teach impedance.

□

# Intentionally

Mistakes
That mistake hurts the mind
How can that be
Done deliberately?
Under the burden of those mistakes
How can the life be lived?

□

## The Skyrocketer

No great work
Anytime and whichever
Can possibly be completed with wile and guile,
The skyrocketer that
Relies on the ground
Never loses it.

□

## New History

Those who from their sweat
Write their intentions,
Only they can change
The lines created in their hands.
The array of jealousy and selfishness
Break with their discretion.
By destroying every obstacle
Climb the tower of success.
Make resolutions everyday
Move ahead in the paths of challenges.
In the pages of the fate
Create new history.

□

## The Gift of Life

Though cannot see you
Have settled you in my mind
At every pulse, at every yearn
Found you in every happiness and sorrow.
Only if we meet for my dream to realise
I wish for the surging world of love,
The song that I have been humming from an era
Let that song be
The greatest gift of life.

□

## At Every Step

Whoever advanced
Has faced
In same proportion the trials.
Hurricane on every side
Thorn in every step
At every step
Has suffered tortures.

□

## Initiative

Friend!
Even we were no less crazy for you,
What do you know that this
Do not know since when
Thought we had.
With hands extended to
You won victory.

□

## Emotions

Ahead of fun
There is no veil,
No substitute
For diligence.
For passion within
To executing something
Even the burning lamps
Scare not of the torrents.

□

## Trust is Being Discounted

Why scared everyone at the crossroads
Who is robbed by the robber,
Moving ahead but following
Why is this confidence broken.

□

## The Pinnacle of Target

Till last breath
There is no logic of fear
Choose to move ahead
You will achieve the pinnacle of your target
Those who ignore you
Will not get anything
But envy and exasperation

□

## Smile

Smile
Allow life to smile too,
Even a moment of it
Do not let go futile
Allow every season of happiness
In this life.

□

# Trust on Them

Why to trust,
Why to die even for them
Those who change with time
Trust and trust
Only those
Whose contemplations
Lived the same way still
When your time was changed.

□

# My Wish

The ardour for the humankind may pulsate
In every throb of my heart
Let there be a beautiful person within me.
Only desire to fulfill in this life
To die for the country
And my life
Be the emblem for humanity.

□

# Surrounded By

I have crushed myself every moment
Surrounded by conflicts,
Of an associate and the stranger
Anguished by the grief and sorrows.

□

## Satisfaction

Hark!
What you have
Share
For the satisfaction
Of your soul
Make every person happy.

□

## The Envy

Like wheezing wheat
Like worms clothing
Similarly jealousy man
Termites the termite
Similarly jealousy
Makes hollow the preposterous.

□

## The Straw

Just not, like that one encounters the destination
Passion has to be awakened,
The emotions of life and death
Have to be attached to the heart
After many flights the birds
Make their nests,
Look at their emotions
They bring the straw in their beaks.

□

## The Shadow

Until the light is in your life
The whole world connects with you
Otherwise, in the darkness
Even the shadow leaves the self.

□

## The Fascination

Fascination, the malady,
The sorrow,
The lament,
A foe of the body,
Besides with the mind.
Weakens the human
Giving birth to many ailments
Snatches the happiness of life.

□

## The Earth

As long as
One is connected to the earth
It paves way for the journey
But if one leaves the land, then
One hardly gets a space to stand on this earth.

□

# The Cowardice

To be scared of change
And
To tremble at struggles
Is cowardice always.

□

# The Anger

This anger is also
Like
A spleen of matchbox
Before ruining others
Wrecks oneself
In the dust.
Erases
Oneself
Fumes and screams,
Rocks the generation for centuries.

□

## No Time for Hatred

I do not have time for hatred
Nor do I have intention for this.
Whoever hates me
I have an affinity for them as well,
I am busy in them
One who loves me unconditionally,
Who are always afraid to hate
We also die with them always.

□

## The Self-Stops

The karma of our actions
Every person enjoys himself
The weakening links and
Opposite winds
He himself stops.

□

## Die Only Once

Die
Will everyone here
Not often
Have to die once
When one has to die
Then, why to be scared in life.

A man in ignorance
Do not know why, everyday
Bit by bit dies,
Desperate sometimes, sometimes frustrated
Is afraid at every step.
You
Neither in disappointment, nor in despair
Just live in liveliness
So that, you
Can give life to others
Just
Drink that nectar.

□

## The Anger

One who has as much the pain
Is as much silent,
May appear on the outside peaceful though
Has netted a lot of resentment within.

□

## My Silence

Do not underestimate
My silence,
My simplicity
As my cowardice,
Growing up within me
Are many notions
Clenched in my silence
For you
Are many a modest questions.

□

## The Beautiful

Ahh! How beautiful is
The life heavenly
But,
At a slight mistake
Life becomes an abyss.

If there is bustle
Let it happen,
If there is colour like heena
Let it be applied.

□

## Say Something

What ensued to you
Say something
Why are you quiet
For a moment though
Open up your mouth.

□

## Not Forever

Why bother
The sun of truth
Can never set,
The darkness
Meant to cheer up the owls and bats
Cannot stop the path of eternity.

□

## With Love

Without awareness of love
Ego is not destroyed
Love is an inspiration
Fills light in life,
Man loses in love
Wins in love.

□

## The Darkness is Going

Look in front
The exposer of truth
The sun of truth
Is coming
Abashed and
Enshrouded in the sheet of despair–
Look! the darkness is going.

□

## Happiness

**(One)**

Happiness
Is limitless, is unique
Is unwise
Is beautiful, the most beautiful.

Everything is zilch
In front of the ultimate
He is Supreme.

**(Two)**

Happiness
Is always in the present
Not in the future,
It is present
In some depths of the mind.

□

## The Feeling of Happiness

Only
About happiness
Mere thinking about happiness will not fetch it
Nor its thriving in your heart
Will be able to fulfill desires.
The feeling of happiness
Is felt in the action to achieve it
The realisation of happiness is in
Reaching the infinite of the journey and its halt.
Only then fragrant life form
And its beautiful flower blossoms
And with its smell
The whole world blossoms.

□

## The Biggest Mistake

Even the desires
Are born
Themselves
Where does they come on
Their own?

In life travelogue
Holding on to the
Desires
Is the biggest mistake,
If you do not abandon them
It is bristly
At each step.

□

# I am the One

I am happiness
I am ecstasy
I am the sweetest hymn of life
I am in love, in light
In the abyss, in the heaven
In the breath of the self
In the inhalations
I am the love beam of humility
I am the peace arbour of divinity.

□

## Human Being

Whose shelter is the earth
Space is the soul,
The sky has taken the format of the roof
Nature is the body itself
The creation is the creator
The Trinity is the protector
A beautiful amazing creation
As a human known.

□

## More than the Desire

Do not shy away from labour
Work
And work more.
If you have no desires in return
Can get more than desired.

□

## Your Pain

You
Encompass all your pleasures,
You are the great mercenary of the world
When your craving starts decreasing
Then your pain gradually starts shielding.

□

## Death

Death is certain
Who could stop it
One day it has to come
The one who has come into the world has to go,
Remembering this forever
The present becomes spirited
Stay free from anger and malice
That is what life says.

□

# It is Good to Die

Without patience
Without efforts
Takes birth purposeless.
Turns the back during the war time
Does not give donation
To the petitioner
What can be done
With such a kind
It is better to die
Than to survive.

□

## What Custom

What kind
Of world is this
Other has to pay
For whatever one does,
Induced by the obduracy of Kaikeyi
Only Ram had to live
In exile.

□

## At Every Step

In its limit
Anything is always glorious
On crossing the border
The same thing snatches away the peace.

No matter how good
Is that thing
However gets destroyed.
Then at every step
Brings only trouble.

□

## Is Penurious

One who is penurious towards himself
How will he help others,
Those who are flying high with support
On killing others
He himself will die.

□

## Don't Do Like This

Oops!
Do not do like this
Do not be afraid of obstacles approaching your life
The paths of my struggles
Don't you know?
Then why not contest
The obstacles
Coming in your way.

□

## Reshuffling

Just watch!
After making some changes in your life
Again not, try bake
The bread already baked.

□

## Strike

Your insensitiveness
Can kill many people
They are dying bit by bit
To pay the price of your ego.

Your dogmas
Desire to remain so-called big
Chastise people
The stones at your path even
Narrate a truth about you.

□

## Not Noticed

Somebody here
Somebody there
But where are
Mine own
Someone here
Understand me,
Know me
Hardly notice
Anyone.

□

## The Curse

If you desire for someone
Find him in your heart
Just
Do not speak anything,
If you need to show the anger
Do it with you tongue,
Just do not fill your heart with
The curse.

□

## Never

Do not be angry
This is the time
If it is lost,
Even if you try it many times
The time lost
Will never be found again.

□

## Only Things

Do not try to change others
If we change, the world will change,
Do not worry only
If we improve, the world will improve.
Things of renunciation alone
Can not bring change
If we are resolute enough and strong
Affection will spill itself from the world.

□

## The Pleasant Game

Sometimes desperate
Sometimes desolation
Sorrow is unlimited, shadow foggy
The games are strange
In this world in a different way
The joys of happiness
Ever meet us in the path
This is the confluence of life
Hopeless despair
Only here is found
The real definition of life.

□

# The Form of Power

Oh Man! You in this world
Are only particles of God
An this earth,
You are a form of supernatural power.

□

## The Lamp

The sun says if I do not stay,
Who will smash the darkness
Who will light the world
When it covers in pitch dark.
In response to this question
Burning a ray of hope
Somewhere away a calm secluded lamp
Exposed the matter of the mind
Do not get frustrated even if you are as sun
Now I opened the door,
I am ready to burn
You just proceed, quipped the lamp

□

## What Happens

Good and bad too
Human being is himself,
Gets only through efforts
And loses in ignorance.
Hardly does he get anything
Who sleeps deep
Where the flowers for him appear
Who the thorns himself sows.

□

## Will Survive

Continuously flowing, genuine desires
Are ours
In every moment to self-absorb
Desire is sweet
Whatever work done, absorbing every moment
Those memories will remain,
The stories of our struggle will tell you
Something.

□

## Cruelty

Infiltrates the house today
Breaks unity
Breaking that
Which every moment connects us.

Trampling down feelings
Raising a havoc
Why remained you uninformed
This cruelty is spreading over every moment.

Much is already happened
Cannot stay silent now
This spreading cruelty
Can not see.

The finishing sensitiveness
To save every moment
Today we have decided
To eradicate this cruelty.

□

## The Unfortunate

There is misfortune in this world
Besides wrong doings
No one is ours even in trouble
Even after death
No one sheds a tear.

□

## As It Is

One gets
What he thinks
By searching for the same
He becomes the same

Thus, it is important
That we think well,
Every moment in our life
We think well.

In this quest
Your personality will become perfect,
In right direction and right thinking
The viewpoint will be the best.

□

## Without Death

God loves
Those only
Who love God
Which only
Pretend to love
Who crave every moment
For love in life.

□

## The Echoes of Duty

True! Life is difficult
For the virtuous
However, the goal is not
Far away,
Like wise
The dutiful does not miss
The echoes of duty.

□

## The Success

Success is begotten
Through every action
Do some work.
Life is very beautiful
Live it with a passion,
Sadly, frustrated, dejected and depressed
Do not lead your life
Become obsessive with all your work
Execute it to the end.

□

## Beautiful Creation

God, while creating man
Wonder what all he must have thought,
A beautiful composition as it is
Must have infused with love as well.
The love that remains huddled within man
Will give life to others,
And every moment in the other
He will discover himself.

□

## If You Can See

If you can see
See something
Within
Yourself
Definitely it will be
Known to you.
Just watch
To get it
To what extent
Your hard work goes.

□

## Accusations

For their own interests
Not less
But loaded me with many blames,
Conspired, oppressed no less
Too many have lain,
They have tried so much
To crush, but still
We have always extended
Our steps forward.

□